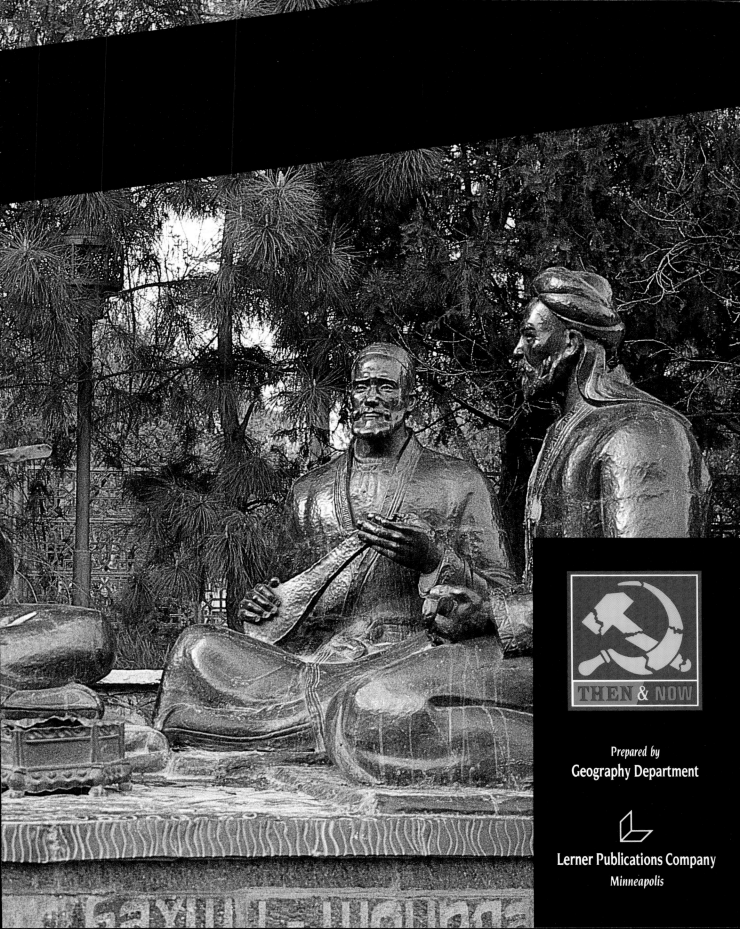

Prepared by
Geography Department

Lerner Publications Company
Minneapolis

Series editors: Mary M. Rodgers, Tom Streissguth,
  Colleen Sexton
Photo researcher: Bill Kauffmann
Designer: Zachary Marell

Our thanks to the following people for their help in
preparing and checking the text of this book: Dr. Craig
ZumBrunnen, Department of Geography, University of
Washington; Vikki Shane, Department of Uralic and Altaic
Studies, Indiana University.

Pronunciation Guide

Esmail	ihs-mah-EEL
Genghis	GEN-giss
glasnost	GLAZ-nost
Khorezm	kho-REZ-ihm
Kyrgyzstan	keer-geez-STAN
Meskhetian	mes-KEH-tee-uhn
muezzin	moo-EZ-ihn
Muynak	mooee-NAHK
Shiite	SHEE-iyt
Sogdiana	sohg-dee-AHN-ah
Zoroastrian	zor-uh-WAHS-tree-uhn

Terms in **bold** appear in a glossary that starts on page 52.

LIBRARY OF CONGRESS CATALOGING-IN-PUBLICATION DATA

Uzbekistan / prepared by Geography Department, Lerner
  Publications Company.
    p. cm. — (Then & now)
  Includes index.
  Summary: Discusses the topography, location, ethnic
mixture, history, and current political situation of the former
Soviet republic of Uzbekistan.
  ISBN 0-8225-2812-6 (lib. bdg.)
  1. Uzbekistan—Juvenile literature. [1. Uzbekistan.] I. Lerner
Publications Company. Geography Dept. II. Series: Then & now
(Minneapolis, Minn.)
DK948.66.U93 1993
958.7—dc20   92-33081
                                             CIP
                                             AC

Manufactured in the United States of America

1 2 3 4 5 6 98 97 96 95 94 93

• CONTENTS •

In Samarkand, an ancient city in southeastern Uzbekistan, a woman carries large, round loaves of freshly baked bread.

"Democracy is the first step, but what comes after that is a big question"

Abdulrahim Pulatov
Leader, Birlik party

In 1992, the Soviet Union would have celebrated the 75th anniversary of the revolution of 1917. During that revolt, political activists called **Communists** overthrew the czar (ruler) and the government of the **Russian Empire.** The revolution of 1917 was the first step in establishing the 15-member **Union of Soviet Socialist Republics (USSR).**

The Soviet Union stretched from eastern Europe across northern Asia and contained nearly 300 million people. Within this vast nation, the Communist government guaranteed housing, education, health care, and lifetime employment. Communist leaders told farmers and factory workers that Soviet citizens owned all property in common. The new nation quickly **industrialized,** meaning it built many new factories and upgraded existing ones. It also modernized and enlarged its farms. In addition, the USSR created a huge, well-equipped military force that allowed it to become one of the most powerful nations in the world.

Schoolchildren visit a memorial in Tashkent, the Uzbek capital, that is dedicated to the courage of the city's residents during a severe earthquake in 1966. The disaster destroyed most of Tashkent, and groups from all over the former Soviet Union helped to rebuild the city.

A worker trims trees near the historic buildings in Registan Square, which dates to about the 15th century. Samarkand lies along the ancient Silk Road —an overland caravan route that brought goods from Asia to the Middle East and Europe.

A wall of colorful tiles in Samarkand's Registan Square dwarfs a young Uzbek. Words on the tiles are written in Arabic, the alphabet in which the Uzbek language appeared until the Cyrillic alphabet was introduced in the mid-20th century.

By the early 1990s, the Soviet Union was in a period of rapid change and turmoil. The central government had mismanaged the economy, which was failing to provide goods. To control the various ethnic groups within the USSR, the Communists had long restricted many freedoms. People throughout the vast nation were dissatisfied.

Several of the republics were seeking independence from Soviet rule—a development that worried some old-style Communists. In August 1991, these conservative Communists tried to use Soviet military power to overthrow the nation's president. Their effort failed and hastened the breakup of the USSR.

The leaders of Uzbekistan, one of five Soviet republics in central Asia, did not rush to proclaim independence from the Soviet Union. For years, Uzbek officials had been seeking more control over agriculture, mining, and local affairs. Nevertheless, as the Soviet Union disintegrated in September 1991, Uzbekistan eventually joined other member-republics in declaring self-rule.

The new Uzbek government, which is headed by a former Communist, has been slow to adopt reforms. Many Uzbeks are becoming impatient for economic, social, and political changes. Unemployment is increasing, and tension among the country's ethnic groups is on the rise. Uzbekistan's leaders must provide a stable political transition, as well as economic growth, to satisfy their citizens' desires for improvements in the nation's living standard.

Flowers (above) *and melons* (right) *are among the items offered at markets throughout Uzbekistan.*

CHAPTER ONE

The Land and People of Uzbekistan

Uzbekistan is a land of vast deserts, broad plains, fertile valleys, and snowcapped mountains. Located in central Asia, the country covers 173,552 square miles (449,500 square kilometers)—an area that is roughly the size of California or Spain.

Four other former Soviet republics in central Asia nearly surround Uzbekistan. Turkmenistan borders Uzbekistan in the southwest. Kazakhstan lies to the west and north, and Kyrgyzstan and Tajikistan are in the east. To the south is Afghanistan, a separate nation that is now struggling to recover from a Soviet invasion and years of civil war.

Uzbekistan holds more people than any other former Soviet republic in central Asia. The country has a high rate of population growth, as well as a large number of citizens who are under the age of 15. This Uzbek family, with the grandfather and grandmother in the center, has more than 100 members.

In northwestern Uzbekistan is the **Karakalpak Autonomous Republic**, a region created by the Soviets in 1932 and inhabited by the Karakalpak people. Dominated by deserts and the Aral Sea, the autonomous republic also has small, fertile areas that support cotton and the raising of cattle and Karakul sheep.

• Topography and Climate •

Uzbekistan has a variety of terrains at many elevations. The northwestern section of the country includes the Ustyurt Plateau, the Kyzyl Kum Desert, and the delta plain of the Amu Darya (*Darya* means "river" in Persian). The Ustyurt Plateau, which extends into Kazakhstan, varies in elevation from 656 to 1,640 feet (200 to 500 meters) above sea level. The Kyzyl Kum Desert features patches of grass and shrubs amid huge amounts of sand.

The foothills and peaks of the Tien and Hissar-Alai mountain systems stretch from southern and eastern Uzbekistan into Kyrgyzstan and Tajikistan. Mount Beshtor—Uzbekistan's highest point—reaches 14,104 feet (4,299 m) above sea level in the Tien range.

Fertile valleys and irrigated plains mark southern, central, and eastern areas of the country. The major valleys are the Zeravshan in central Uzbekistan, the Chirchik in the northeast, and the Fergana in the east. These areas contain good soil and are intensively farmed.

Uzbekistan's many rivers and canals benefit agriculture and the country's energy industry. Dams and canals direct water from the Syr Darya, the Amu Darya, and the Zeravshan River to farmland and hydroelectric stations. Among the major artificial waterways are the Great Fergana Canal and the Kara Kum Canal.

(Above) *Kids splash and swim in the Amu Darya (River) as it flows toward the Aral Sea in northwestern Uzbekistan.* (Below) *Scattered shrubs dot the landscape of the Kyzyl Kum Desert.*

(Above) **Canals bring water to dry areas throughout the country.** (Below) **Herders raise sheep and goats in the Zeravshan Valley of central Uzbekistan.**

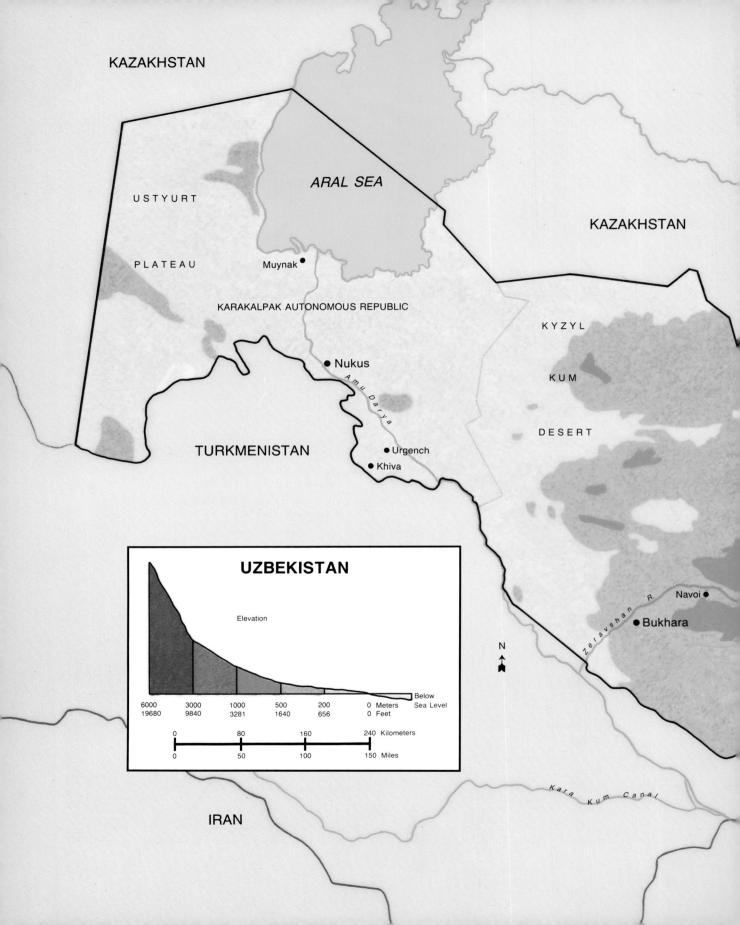

KAZAKHSTAN

KAZAKHSTAN

ARAL SEA

USTYURT

PLATEAU

Muynak ●

KARAKALPAK AUTONOMOUS REPUBLIC

KYZYL

KUM

DESERT

● Nukus

Amu Darya

TURKMENISTAN

● Urgench

● Khiva

Navoi ●

Zeravshan R.

● Bukhara

N

IRAN

Kara Kum Canal

UZBEKISTAN

Elevation

| 6000 | 3000 | 1000 | 500 | 200 | 0 | Meters |
| 19680 | 9840 | 3281 | 1640 | 656 | 0 | Feet |

Below
Sea Level

0   80   160   240   Kilometers

0   50   100   150   Miles

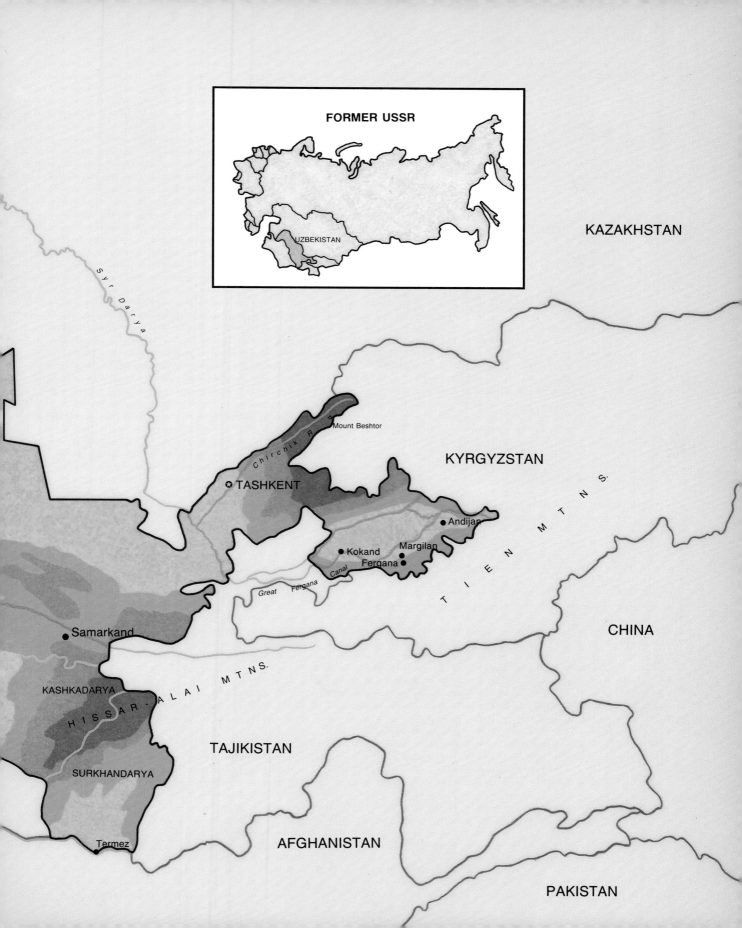

FORMER USSR

UZBEKISTAN

KAZAKHSTAN

Syr Darya

Chirchik R. Mount Beshtor

KYRGYZSTAN

✪ TASHKENT

• Andijan

• Kokand   Margilan
          Fergana •

Canal
Great   Fergana

T I E N   M T N S.

CHINA

• Samarkand

H I S S A R - A L A I   M T N S.

KASHKADARYA

TAJIKISTAN

SURKHANDARYA

AFGHANISTAN

• Termez

PAKISTAN

Young Uzbeks play on a fishing boat stranded by the receding shores of the Aral Sea.

Uzbekistan's lakes are located in the valleys and deltas of its main rivers. The Aral Sea—once the world's fourth largest lake—crosses Uzbekistan's northwestern border with Kazakhstan. To irrigate farmland, Soviet engineers diverted river water that flowed into this sea. As a result, the Aral Sea is slowly evaporating. Experts believe that this body of water could disappear within the next 30 years.

Uzbekistan experiences moderately cold winters and very hot summers. The average temperature in January, the coldest month, ranges from 18° F (−8° C) on the Ustyurt Plateau to 37° F (3° C) in the south. In July, the hottest month, temperatures average 79° F (26° C) in the north and 86° F (30° C) in the south. In the desert, the temperature of the sand can rise to 158° F (70° C) on hot summer days.

Scant amounts of rain—as little as 4 inches (10 centimeters)—fall annually in the lowlands of Uzbekistan. Mountainous areas receive up to 24 inches (61 cm) of precipitation per year, much of which is snow. Along Uzbekistan's border with Afghanistan, a strong, dry wind called the **afghanets** (the Russian word for "Afghan") arrives from the southwest. The dusty, dirty gusts of the afghanets—which blow for nearly 70 days each year in the winter and spring—clog machinery with grit and force people to cover their faces when they are outside.

Pomegranate trees, whose red fruit can be processed into pomegranate juice, thrive in the hot, fertile valleys of eastern Uzbekistan.

An Uzbek woman covers her face against the gritty blasts of a sandstorm.

• *Cities* •

Uzbekistan contains many cities of more than 100,000 people. A number of these hubs were founded centuries ago and have turbulent histories. About 40 percent of the nation's 21.3 million people live in urban areas.

Tashkent (population 2.1 million), the capital of Uzbekistan, is an industrial, educational, and commercial center in the northeastern part of the country. A very old city, Tashkent has yielded human artifacts from roughly 300,000 years ago. In 1966, Tashkent's historic structures suffered severe damage from a very strong earthquake. The rebuilding of the capital has given it a modern appearance. Factories in Tashkent make agricultural machinery, aircraft, textiles, and footwear. The capital also hosts the Uzbek Academy of Sciences and the University of Tashkent.

In Tashkent, a huge poster carries the word peace *in many languages. Although the city has been inhabited for roughly 2,000 years, rebuilding since the 1966 earthquake has given Tashkent a modern look.*

A *member of* Uzbekistan's ethnic Korean population sells rice at a market in Tashkent.

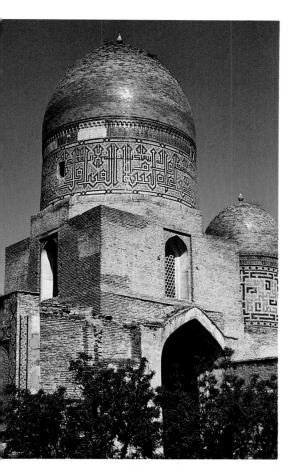

Unlike Tashkent, Samarkand has many ancient structures, including the Shakhi-Zinda Mausoleum. This above-ground tomb holds the remains of an Arab missionary who helped to bring the Islamic faith to central Asia in the 8th century.

Located in the Zeravshan River Valley, Samarkand (population 370,000) is one of the oldest settlements in central Asia. The city has seen the armies of the Greek king Alexander the Great and of the Mongol warrior Genghis Khan, who completely destroyed the city in 1220. A later Mongol commander named Timur rebuilt Samarkand, which still holds many beautiful mosques (Islamic places of worship), madrasas (Islamic schools), and mausoleums (above-ground tombs).

A major educational center, Samarkand is the home of the University of Samarkand and the Karakul Institute. Under Soviet rule, Samarkand's industries were expanded to include silk-weaving factories, fruit-canning plants, and tea-curing businesses.

An overview (above) *of Samarkand shows the domes and towers of this historic city. Registan Square is famous for its three ornate buildings, all of which were once madrasas (Islamic schools). A detail* (below) *from the doorway of the Shir-Dar Madrasa features tigers chasing deer.*

According to Uzbek tradition, women braid their hair in two thick plaits, while girls, such as these residents of the city of Bukhara, twist their long, dark tresses into as many as 40 thin braids.

With a population of 228,000, Bukhara is an economic and energy hub in the Zeravshan Valley. The city boasts large dairy, meat, textile, and wine-making enterprises, as well as smaller businesses that produce traditional handicrafts, such as rugs and metalware. A center of the Islamic religion, Bukhara contains important mosques and mausoleums.

Nukus (population 175,000), the capital of the Karakalpak Autonomous Republic, has factories that refine cotton, assemble clothing, make building materials, and process meat and dairy products. The city's major school, the University of Karakalpakia, was founded in 1976.

Buyers and sellers negotiate prices at a market in Nukus, the capital of the Karakalpak Autonomous Republic.

• *Ethnic Heritage* •

Ethnic Uzbeks make up 71 percent of Uzbekistan's population. The ancestors of the Uzbeks were central Asian nomads who conquered the region in the 1500s. For centuries after the takeover, the Uzbeks intermarried with the region's settled peoples. The newcomers learned to grow crops while pursuing their traditional livelihood of raising livestock.

In the late 19th century, when the Russian Empire expanded into central Asia, many Russians moved to the region. **Ethnic Russians** now form approximately 8 percent of Uzbekistan's population. Since the country's independence in 1991, however, thousands of Russians have returned to Russia—a migration that has caused shortages of skilled labor in many industries.

Central Asian Turkic peoples—such as Kazakhs, Turkmen, and Kyrgyz—together form roughly 5 percent of Uzbekistan's population. Another 4 percent are Tajiks, a Persian-speaking, non-Turkic people who also inhabit Tajikistan and Afghanistan. The Karakalpaks, the majority in the Karakalpak Autonomous Republic, make up 2 percent of the total population. Small numbers of Koreans, Tatars, Ukrainians, Armenians, Arabs, and Belarussians complete Uzbekistan's ethnic mixture.

• *Language* •

Under Soviet rule, both Uzbek and Russian were official languages in Uzbekistan. Since independence, Uzbek alone has been the country's official language, and fluency in this Turkic tongue is now a requirement for holding a government post. Most of the Russians who live in Uzbekistan chose not to learn Uzbek. They fear that, without knowledge of Uzbek, they might lose their jobs.

(Above) *At Andijan, an industrial city near Uzbekistan's eastern border, a boy wears an embroidered skullcap while playing with a ball and stick.* (Below) *A young Karakalpak poses outside his family's home near the Aral Sea.*

Most ethnic Russian school-children in Uzbekistan have not learned to speak Uzbek.

Since independence, signs in Uzbekistan have appeared in Arabic as well as in the Cyrillic lettering used for Russian.

Scholars used the Arabic alphabet to write Uzbek until the early 20th century, when the Soviets imposed the Latin alphabet throughout Soviet central Asia. At about the same time, the Turks adopted the Latin alphabet to write Turkish. Concerned that Soviet central Asians might develop deeper ties with Turkey, the Soviet government required the use of the Cyrillic alphabet in 1940. Cyrillic, in which the Russian language appears, became the means for writing all Turkic languages spoken in the Soviet Union. This imposed change was one of the ways in which the Soviets tried to **Russify** central Asian peoples.

The government of Uzbekistan has not yet decided on an alphabet for modern written Uzbek. Uzbek schools and publications have begun to use the Arabic script. As Uzbekistan develops closer relations with Turkey and with nations in Europe, however, Uzbek leaders may favor adopting the Latin alphabet.

• Religion and Festivals •

Until the Arab conquest of the 8th century A.D., the peoples of Uzbekistan followed many different religions. These ancient beliefs survive in the Persian (Iranian) New Year's festival, which is celebrated each March on the first day of spring. On New Year's Eve, Uzbeks light bonfires, sing traditional songs, and recite poetry.

The Arabs converted Uzbeks, other Turkic peoples, and Tajiks to the Sunni form of the Islamic religion. The followers of Islam, called Muslims, must fulfill several obligations. Devout Muslims, for example, pray five times daily, make donations to the poor, and fast during the holy month of Ramadan.

Although the Soviet government discouraged religious practices, people of all faiths continued to observe rituals related to birth, marriage, and burial. Since independence, the Uzbek government has lifted most religious restrictions. Muslims now openly celebrate the holiday that ends Ramadan, and the Uzbek Academy of Sciences has put together the first Uzbek-language version of the Koran (the Muslim holy book).

Although the majority of people in Uzbekistan are Muslims, other religions are practiced. The Russians brought Russian Orthodox Christianity, and members of Uzbekistan's Korean population follow Buddhism. The country also has a small Jewish community.

• Education and Health •

The Uzbek government guarantees the nation's children an education. Primary school usually lasts

(Above) *Wearing a traditional white turban, a mullah (Islamic teacher) enjoys a cup of green tea.* (Below) *With hands outstretched in prayer, Muslims (followers of Islam) participate in religious services while facing Mecca, Saudi Arabia, the birthplace of Muhammad, Islam's founder.*

Science is part of the course-work at this school near Tash-kent.

nine years, followed by two or three years of secondary school. Some vocational institutions provide both secondary education and job training. About 98 percent of the population can read and write.

Uzbekistan has several postsecondary institutions. The University of Tashkent and the University of Samarkand offer courses in math, physics, history, foreign languages, and journalism. Other schools train students in the latest agricultural, medical, and scientific technologies.

The Soviet government set up a free, comprehensive health-care system, much of which is still in place. The cost of this system, however, is now borne by the independent Uzbek state. Some common medicines are in short supply, and specialized care and skilled personnel are not always available. In addition, the country's high birthrate and growing youthful population puts added pressure on the national health-care system.

A major health concern for Uzbekistan is the impact of the Aral Sea's decline on the Karakalpak population. The life expectancy for people in Karakalpak villages is about 42 years. For the population as a whole, that figure is 69 years. The country's overall infant mortality rate is high—64 deaths in every 1,000 live births. For people living near the Aral Sea, the figure is four times higher. Contaminated drinking water has caused deadly outbreaks of typhoid, cholera, and hepatitis among Karakalpaks.

Irrigation projects are decreasing the availability of safe drinking water in the Karakalpak Autonomous Republic. In addition, farm fertilizers and other chemicals have poisoned the remaining water, which many Karakalpak families use for cooking, bathing, and drinking. As a result, cases of typhoid and hepatitis have increased in the region.

CHAPTER TWO

Uzbekistan's Story

Many groups have passed through Uzbekistan during its long and eventful history. The country's location in central Asia made it a natural choice for trade routes linking eastern Asia, the Middle East, and southern Europe. Because of these historical ties, modern Uzbekistan continues to be a commercial crossroads with a mixed ethnic heritage.

• The Pre-Islamic Era •

Archaeological evidence shows that humans have lived in Uzbekistan since prehistoric times. Early inhabitants hunted and gathered their food until about 2000 B.C., when the first settled, agricultural societies developed. Farmers bred sheep, cattle, and horses and irrigated the land to grow wheat, barley, and millet. In mountainous regions, where little cropland was available, the raising of livestock was particularly important.

A monument in Samarkand exhibits the dazzling tilework that is typical of many of the city's buildings. Islamic tradition discourages the use of human figures in art, so designers developed elaborate geometric patterns to decorate madrasas and mosques (Islamic places of worship).

As villagers continued to follow this peaceful lifestyle, the area of modern Uzbekistan became part of several ancient Persian states, including Bactria in the south and Khorezm in the northwest. The capital of the kingdom of Sogdiana was at Maracanda (Samarkand) in the southeast. Each of these realms had its own religion and culture.

By the 6th century B.C., central Asia had come under the authority of Cyrus the Great, the first king of Persia's (modern Iran's) Achaemenid dynasty (family of rulers). Cyrus introduced the Zoroastrian religion and expanded the Persian Empire's borders far to the west and east. His successors, however, failed to maintain a hold on this vast domain.

In the early fourth century B.C., Alexander the Great of Greece invaded central Asia and overthrew

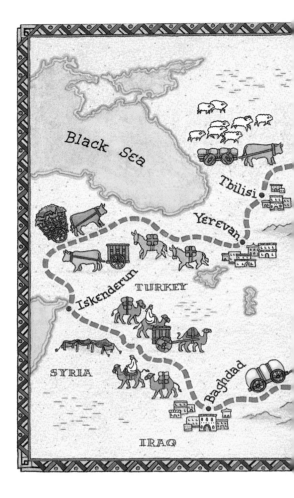

An illustration shows the marriage procession of Alexander the Great and the Bactrian princess Roxana in 327 B.C. After Alexander's death in 323 B.C., Roxana went to Macedonia, her husband's homeland, whose new king Cassander eventually ordered her execution.

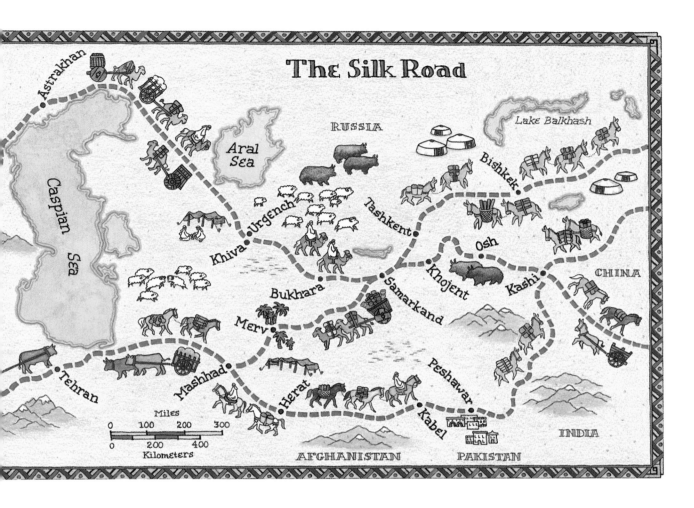

The Silk Road

Linking China and Europe, the 4,000-mile (6,400-km) Silk Road thrived from the 2nd century B.C. to the 8th century A.D. Caravans brought fine silk fabric westward, while horses, glass, wool, gold, and silver made the journey eastward. Few merchants traveled the entire route. Instead, using camels, oxen, donkeys, and horses, goods moved steadily from city to city with the help of local brokers. Tashkent, Samarkand, Urgench, Khiva, and Bukhara were stops on the Silk Road.

Achaemenid rule. His conquest—and his marriage to Roxana, a Bactrian princess—brought Greek influences to Uzbekistan. After Alexander's death in 323 B.C., his dynasty crumbled. Alexander's generals then divided his empire, with Seleucus taking the old Persian lands in central Asia.

The Seleucid kingdom lasted only a few centuries. By about the 1st century A.D., the Kushan people of the Hindu Kush Mountains of northern Afghanistan had pushed into Uzbekistan. Kushan kings adopted the faith of Buddhism and spread its message of peace and religious tolerance. The Kushan Empire's economy depended on peaceful trade and on the overland caravan routes between southern Europe, the Middle East, and eastern Asia. For several hundred years, Uzbekistan thrived under the Kushan. Traditional arts and handicrafts flourished, and trade with various countries expanded.

This peaceful existence was shattered by an invasion of nomadic Turks in the 6th century A.D. The Turks, who came from the northeast, seized the Kushan Empire's valuable caravan routes and took control of most of its cities. After settling in the agricultural areas of Uzbekistan, the Turks slowly changed their nomadic way of life and turned to farming and trade.

• The Coming of Islam •

Another invasion occurred in the 8th century, when Arab warriors arrived from the Middle East. After conquering central Asia, they introduced the religion of Islam, which the region's people strongly resisted. In their drive to convert the inhabitants, the Arabs seized several cities, including Bukhara and Samarkand. Swayed by the force of both the Arab army and the Islamic message, the people of Uzbekistan gradually accepted the Islamic faith.

The vast Arab Empire, which stretched from North Africa to India, was too big to govern without the help of local leaders. In the 9th century, Samankhoda, a Persian noble who worked for the Arabs, founded the Samanid dynasty with Bukhara as its capital. Under Samanid rule, Samarkand, Termez, Khorezm, and Tashkent became major commercial, religious, and educational centers. Caravans continued to travel through Uzbekistan, bringing leather goods, silk, wool, and livestock to and from areas as far north as the Baltic Sea.

Samanid power waned at the end of the 10th century. As a result, new independent kingdoms

Uzbekistan was an intellectual and commercial crossroads in the 9th and 10th centuries, during the reign of the Samanids. One of the country's most famous citizens was Ibn Sina (called Avicenna in Europe), who was born in Bukhara in A.D. 980. By the time he was 18, Ibn Sina was already regarded as a learned doctor and philosopher and had become the court physician of the Samanid ruler. Here, Ibn Sina (at back in orange hat) *is pictured with Galen and Hippocrates—ancient Greek writers of medical works.*

Dating to 1127, the Kalyan Minaret (tower) in Bukhara is 155 feet (47 meters) tall. Its exterior is made of soft terra-cotta clay laid on thick alabaster stone. From this height, four muezzins (Islamic callers) announced Friday prayers. The minaret also served as a watch-tower for incoming caravans or invaders. When the Mongol commander Genghis Khan reached Bukhara in the early 13th century, he ordered everything in the city to be destroyed except the Kalyan Minaret.

emerged, including the Ghaznavid state in what is now southern Uzbekistan and the Khorezm state in the northwest. By the late 1100s, Khorezm had become the most powerful domain in central Asia.

• New Conquerors •

Khorezm's power was short lived. In the early 13th century, a huge army of Mongol warriors arrived in the region from Asia. Guided by their leader Genghis Khan, the Mongols attacked in 1220, killing much of the population and destroying cities, farms, and irrigation works.

In the late 1300s, Genghis's descendant Timur (known in Europe as Tamerlane) used his armies to conquer territory from the Black Sea in the west to India in the east. Bukhara became the Timurid Empire's religious and educational hub, while Samarkand was its capital city.

After Timur's death in 1405, Mongol power declined, enabling other groups to establish themselves in the region. In the late 15th and early 16th centuries, a Turkic people called the Uzbeks invaded and conquered central Asia under the leadership of Muhammad Shaybani.

As the Uzbeks replaced the Mongols, the Safavid dynasty came to power in Persia. Shah Esmail, the founder of the Safavids, established the Shiite form of the Islamic faith as his state's religion. The Uzbeks, who followed the Sunni branch, fought many religious wars with the Persians. In 1510, during one of these conflicts, Muhammad Shaybani was killed.

The Gur Emir Mausoleum (left) *houses the remains of Timur* (above), *the Mongol leader who rebuilt Bukhara and conquered areas far beyond the borders of Uzbekistan. Born near Samarkand in 1336, Timur was a skilled and ruthless commander as well as a patron of the arts.*

Nevertheless, the Uzbeks, under the Shaybanid dynasty, held on to their land and their Sunni faith.

Gradually, the Uzbeks became settled farmers, cultivating crops and intermarrying with the local population. The region's cities, however, still depended on overland trade to make money. In the 1500s, European merchants and explorers found routes to Asia by sea. As the caravan trails lost favor, commerce in central Asia declined.

Floral and geometric mosaics decorate a building in Khiva, an ancient city that was destroyed by the Mongols. A thriving trade in slaves helped Khiva to prosper again in the early 16th century. The city's wealth, however, attracted both Uzbek and Persian armies, who fought over the city and surrounding region for several centuries.

The Uzbek leader Muhammad Shaybani battled the Persians for control of Uzbekistan in the early 1500s. His success laid the foundation of the Uzbek state in central Asia.

Weakened by the loss of trade, the Uzbek Empire broke into states called **khanates,** each of which was headed by a **khan** (prince). The khanates of Bukhara and Khiva emerged in the 16th century, and the khanate of Kokand formed in the 18th century. Frequent wars among the khanates hampered their ability to fend off foreign powers—including the Russian Empire.

• *Russian Rule* •

Centered in Moscow far to the northwest, Russia had begun to move its well-equipped armies into southern and central Asia. Invasions in the early 19th century allowed Russia to **annex** (take over) land from the Turks and the Persians. In 1865, Russian forces seized Tashkent (part of Kokand). Samarkand and Bukhara were captured in 1868, and Khiva fell in 1873.

Russia's success forced the khans of both Bukhara and Khiva to sign peace treaties that made these two khanates Russian **protectorates,** meaning the empire pledged to safeguard them from attack. The Russian czar (ruler) abolished Kokand in 1876 and added its territory to **Russian Turkestan.** In the late 1880s, the czar divided the land of present-day Uzbekistan among Turkestan, Khiva, and Bukhara.

In Uzbekistan, the Russians established huge cotton plantations, hoping to compete with the United States in supplying cotton to the international textile industry. The Russians also built new factories that processed raw cotton and other agricultural products.

To transport the cotton, the Russians built railway lines that connected central Asia's major cities to export hubs in Russia. Despite these economic inroads, little cultural change took place in Uzbeki-

The Shaybanid dynasty (family of rulers) made Bukhara the capital of its domain, and the city eventually became an Islamic educational center. This madrasa, which features four towers decorated with blue bricks, is also home to a flock of storks.

stan under Russian rule. Russians moving into the region settled in urban communities away from central Asians. While the Russians introduced wine-making, hog farming, and the Orthodox religion, traditional Uzbek family life and religious practices remained undisturbed.

• Soviet Uzbekistan •

In the early 20th century, the Uzbeks began to resist czarist policies, including a law that gave Uzbek land to Russian farmers. In addition, Russia drafted Uzbeks to fight in World War I (1914–1918), an international conflict that pitted Russia and its allies against Germany and Turkey. To feed the Russian army, the government increased exports of central Asian cotton and cut back on imports of grain and other foods. The shortage of food caused famine in Turkestan and worsened discontent in the region.

The war's hardships were also causing dissatisfaction throughout the empire. In 1917, political activists called Communists led a revolution in Russia that promised workers better wages, more food, and peace. The Russian Revolution toppled the czar and spread to Turkestan. But when Islamic leaders in the region tried to set up an independent government, they were overpowered by the forces of the Tashkent Soviet—the ruling organization set up by Communists in Turkestan.

In the 1860s, the Russian Empire took over Bukhara and other parts of Uzbekistan. To supply a growing textile industry, Russian leaders established huge cotton plantations that employed many workers to pick the fiber of the plant (above). **To transport the raw cotton, the Russians also built railway lines** (left) **that linked Uzbek cities with Russian ports.**

In 1918, the Tashkent Soviet established the **Turkestan Autonomous Soviet Socialist Republic.** Some Uzbeks who opposed this change formed an anti-Soviet resistance group known as the Basmachi movement. Centered in the Fergana Valley, the movement survived until 1926, when the Soviet Red Army defeated it.

In 1924, the Soviet government began the **delimitation** of Turkestan. This process drew new borders that created five central Asian Soviet Socialist Republics (SSRs), including the Uzbek SSR. These republics became part of the larger Union of Soviet Socialist Republics (USSR).

• World War II and Its Aftermath •

In the 1930s and 1940s, the Soviet government sought to increase the cultivation and processing of cotton in Uzbekistan. To accomplish this goal, the Soviets forced private farmers to combine their small holdings into large, state-owned **collective farms.** Many of those who resisted collectivization were imprisoned or executed.

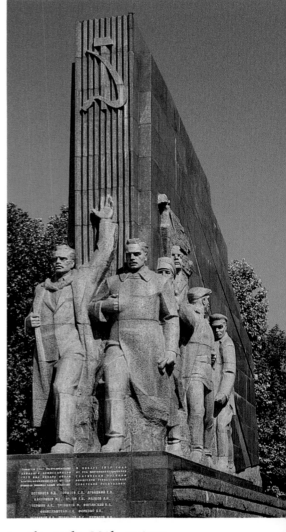

In the early 20th century— when revolutionaries called Communists were trying to make Uzbekistan part of a Soviet state—a street in Tashkent (left) still contained ancient buildings. A monument in Tashkent (above) honors 14 Soviet officials who were killed in an anti-Soviet uprising in 1919. By 1925, the Soviets had established the Uzbek Soviet Socialist Republic.

In the 1940s, the USSR fought in another world war. During the conflict, Joseph Stalin, the country's leader, suspected disloyalty among many of the Soviet Union's ethnic minorities, including the Meskhetian Turks of the Georgian SSR. To strengthen its authority, the Soviet government deported Meskhetian Turks to Uzbekistan, where they formed a small part of the population.

In the decades following World War II (1939–1945), the Soviet government developed heavy industries in Uzbekistan, including machine assembly and textile manufacturing. In addition, engineering projects diverted the waters of the Amu Darya and Syr Darya to irrigate vast cotton fields, causing the gradual shrinking of the Aral Sea. Although new schools and health facilities were built, the government strictly controlled information and travel in the central Asian SSRs.

This map shows that the diversion of inflowing water has caused the shores of the Aral Sea to recede. The diversion began in earnest in the 1950s, when Communist central planners decided that cotton from Uzbekistan should supply the Soviet Union's expanding textile industry. Cotton plants need fertile, well-drained soil and plenty of water—conditions that are not found naturally in western Uzbekistan. By rerouting water from the Amu Darya and Syr Darya, the Soviets fostered a huge cotton industry as well as an ecological disaster.

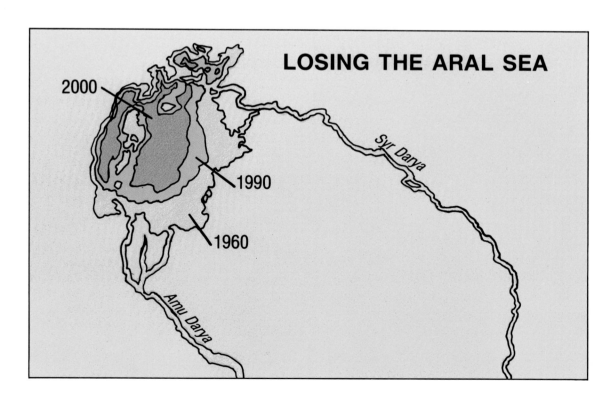

LOSING THE ARAL SEA

2000

1990

1960

Syr Darya

Amu Darya

• *Ethnic Tensions and Independence* •

In the 1980s, the Soviet leader Mikhail Gorbachev introduced the policy of *glasnost*, which means "openness" in the Russian language. This policy allowed freer expressions of opinion, of cultural identity, and of religious beliefs. By permitting debate, however, glasnost also unleashed ethnic tensions that had been building throughout central Asia.

In June 1989, for example, more than 100 people were killed in the Fergana Valley when young Uzbeks attacked Meskhetian Turks in their homes and businesses. One year later, unrest again exploded in the Fergana Valley—this time between Uzbeks and Kyrgyz—and claimed 115 lives.

These and other violent events in the USSR convinced some conservative Soviet leaders that glasnost was threatening their authority. In August 1991, they staged a **coup d'état** to overthrow Gorbachev. Islam Karimov, the head of the Communist party in Uzbekistan, favored the coup leaders at first but later expressed his support for Gorbachev. Anti-coup demonstrations—especially those in Russia—quickly caused the coup to fail. Within days, republics throughout the USSR were declaring independence.

Following the lead of Russia, Ukraine, and other SSRs, Uzbekistan proclaimed self-rule in September 1991. During elections held in December, Uzbek voters chose Karimov as president of Uzbekistan. Like the Soviet regime, Karimov's government continues to control the media and to limit the activities of opposition parties, including the Birlik (meaning "unity") party, the Erk (Free) party, and the Islamic Renaissance party.

These opposition groups are working to dismantle the Communist structure of Karimov's government. They promote the creation of a state that

(Above) *Fires destroyed homes and businesses during ethnic unrest in 1989.* (Below) *Since Uzbekistan declared independence in 1991, it has revived Islamic traditions and is repairing Islamic buildings.*

The new Uzbek flag (left) **flies over a structure in Bukhara that also displays the old emblem of Soviet Uzbekistan.**

guarantees human rights and free elections and that seeks to put economic, social, and environmental reforms in place. These parties also support some degree of Islamic influence on the government. Only the Islam Democratic party favors using **Sharia** (Islamic law) to run the country.

The USSR's 15 member-republics had achieved independence, but this move did not untangle the complex economic and political system set up by the Soviets. Three of the former SSRs—Russia, Ukraine, and Belarus—realized that the new nations needed some type of cooperative group. In early December 1991, they formed the **Commonwealth of Independent States** as a loose economic and military association. Uzbekistan, as well as the rest of the former SSRs of central Asia, joined the commonwealth in late December.

To rebuild Uzbekistan's economy, the country's leaders are trying to obtain international loans and to attract foreign investments. In addition, Islamic states in the region are helping to construct highways and oil pipelines through central Asia. An Uzbek national airline has begun to operate, although its planes often lack fuel and spare parts. Hindering the efforts to improve conditions in Uzbekistan are the country's high unemployment, rising consumer prices, and rapidly increasing population. To achieve stability and prosperity, Uzbek leaders must win the support of democratic reformers as well as of Islamic authorities.

CHAPTER THREE

Making a Living in Uzbekistan

For centuries, Uzbekistan's people depended on livestock breeding, trade, and agriculture to make a living. The country's modern economy has expanded to include heavy industries, mining, and the development of energy resources.

Under Soviet rule, the central government in Moscow controlled the distribution of goods and linked Uzbekistan's activities to the USSR's general economic plan. Independence now allows Uzbeks to set their own economic goals and to find their own foreign markets. The Uzbek government has also proposed laws that lessen restrictions on foreign businesses operating in the country. Uzbek leaders hope that this change will stimulate trade and will encourage new investment from Europe, the Middle East, southeastern Asia, and the United States.

At a cannery in Muynak, a worker fills tins with chopped fish caught in the Caspian Sea. The town was once a major fishing hub on the Aral Sea, which no longer provides fish. As a result, Muynak has declined and must import fish supplies.

During the harvest season, trucks loaded with cotton fiber arrive at processing stations throughout Uzbekistan.

Near Tashkent, a worker cuts heavy bunches of grapes from an overhanging vine.

• Agriculture •

Agriculture, especially the planting of cotton, is the mainstay of Uzbekistan's economy. The country is still one of the world's top producers of cotton, most of which is grown in the northwest, in the east, and along the valley of the Amu Darya. Once called "white gold"—because of the money it earned for the USSR—cotton might now be called "the white plague," because of the massive environmental damage it has brought to the region's water and soil.

Uzbekistan also leads in the cultivation of kenaf, a tough plant used to make rope, sacks, and other heavy materials. Farmers plant kenaf primarily in the Tashkent area. Irrigation helps Uzbek and Karakalpak farmers to grow rice in the east and northwest. Wheat and barley thrive near Samarkand and in the Kashkadarya region, and tobacco fields dot the eastern foothills and mountains.

The fertile valleys of Fergana, Zeravshan, and Chirchik support orchards of apricot, cherry, fig, peach, and pomegranate trees. The vineyards of the Fergana and Tashkent regions produce grapes that are made into wine or sun-dried raisins. Samarkand and Tashkent are famous for vegetables, melons, and gourds (the hollow fruits of gourd plants).

The raising of livestock is important in northern and western Uzbekistan. The country is also a leader in the breeding of Karakul sheep, which come mainly from desert and semidesert areas of Bukhara and Kyzyl Kum. Although Karakul meat is of good quality, most herders raise the sheep for their wool and pelts.

In the foothills and mountainous areas of Uzbekistan, cattle and goats provide meat and dairy products. Chicken farms are common throughout the country, but Koreans and Russians raise most of the pigs because of Islamic restrictions on eating pork. The breeding of horses and camels occurs in western areas of the country. The Karakalpaks raise muskrat, mink, and silver foxes for their fur.

In many parts of the country, Uzbek families raise poultry (above) *for their meat and eggs.* **Uzbek herders value the thick, curly fleece of Karakul lambs** (right), *which can be processed into jackets, coats, and hats.*

THE DECLINE OF THE ARAL SEA

In the 1960s, the town of Muynak in the Karakalpak Autonomous Republic was an important Soviet fishing hub on the shores of the Aral Sea. Since that time, the Aral has shrunk dramatically, and its waters now lie more than 20 miles (32 km) from Muynak. As a result, the town's fishing industry has declined.

The drastic change in the Aral's shoreline followed Soviet efforts to increase cotton production in Uzbekistan. Cotton plants flourish in fertile soil that gets plenty of moisture. Although the dry climate and salty soil of western Uzbekistan are not naturally suited to growing cotton, this did not discourage Soviet planners. They diverted (rerouted) the waters of the Aral Sea's two inflowing rivers —the Amu Darya and the Syr Darya— to irrigation canals. Because less water was available to replace moisture lost through evaporation, the Aral began to shrink and by the early 1990s had lost 40 percent of its surface area. Yields of cotton, however, had doubled.

The diversion of water has caused other environmental and health problems in the region. The soil, for example, is becoming less fertile. Irrigation pushes salt in the soil to the surface, where it forms a thick crust on cotton plants. More than 78 percent of the Karakalpak population are sick from using water that has been poisoned by farm chemicals. Uzbek scientists have proposed ways to return water to the sea. Unless action is taken soon, however, the Aral Sea will disappear within 30 years.

Fishing boats have been stranded by the shrinking Aral Sea.

Uzbekistan's manufacturing and service sectors employ most of the country's work force. Here, a textile laborer monitors machinery in a silk factory in the eastern city of Margilan (below) and a welder repairs a mosque in Tashkent (right).

• Manufacturing and Trade •

Uzbekistan's major industries—which are located mainly in Tashkent, Samarkand, Bukhara, Khiva, and Nukus—are closely tied to the country's agricultural output. Cotton and wool, for example, are the materials for a large textile industry that includes the production of hosiery, knitwear, and leather shoes. The assembly of machines that farmers use to grow, harvest, transport, and process cotton is another key branch of industry. Most agricultural machinery comes from the Tashkent region. Factories in and near Samarkand, Fergana, and Navoi make farm fertilizers.

Smaller industries throughout the country process food, building materials, and silkworms. Workers extract vegetable oil from cotton seeds, can fruit, process fish, and make wine. Local stone is the raw material for producing cement, reinforced concrete blocks, bricks, and shingles throughout Uzbekistan and in the Karakalpak Autonomous Republic. Many families in the Fergana Valley add to their income by raising silkworms, whose cocoons (outer coverings) can be spun into silk fabric.

With its many exportable products, Uzbekistan is heavily dependent on international trade. The country maintains economic ties with republics of the former USSR and with foreign countries. Uzbekistan exports cotton fiber, raw silk, fabrics, Karakul pelts, agricultural machinery, marble, vegetables, grapes, and rice. The country imports petroleum products, lumber, chemical fertilizers, and grain.

• Mining and Energy •

Uzbekistan is rich in mineral resources, including silver, copper, tungsten, and lead. Workers mine gold in the Kyzyl Kum Desert, and deposits of non-metals, such as fluorite, sulfur, limestone, and marble, are also plentiful. Semiprecious stones and gems—such as turquoise, onyx, and garnet—exist in many areas of the country.

Natural gas is Uzbekistan's major energy resource, with the country's largest deposits in the Bukhara region. Through a system of pipelines, Uzbekistan supplies natural gas to its central Asian neighbors, as well as to Russia. Although hydropowered electric plants exist, thermal stations fueled by natural gas generate most of the country's electricity.

Coal mines lie near Tashkent, as well as in the southern Surkhandarya region. Workers extract and refine oil in the Fergana Valley, in the Bukhara region, and in southern areas of the country. Pipelines to Turkey, Iran, and elsewhere are under construction and may increase Uzbekistan's income from this resource.

Most urban Uzbeks work in factories (above), *some of which get their electricity from hydropower stations* (below).

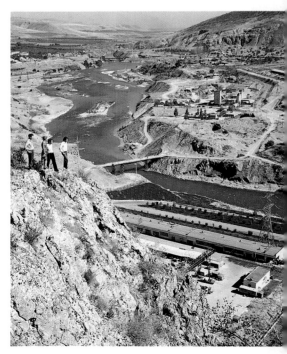

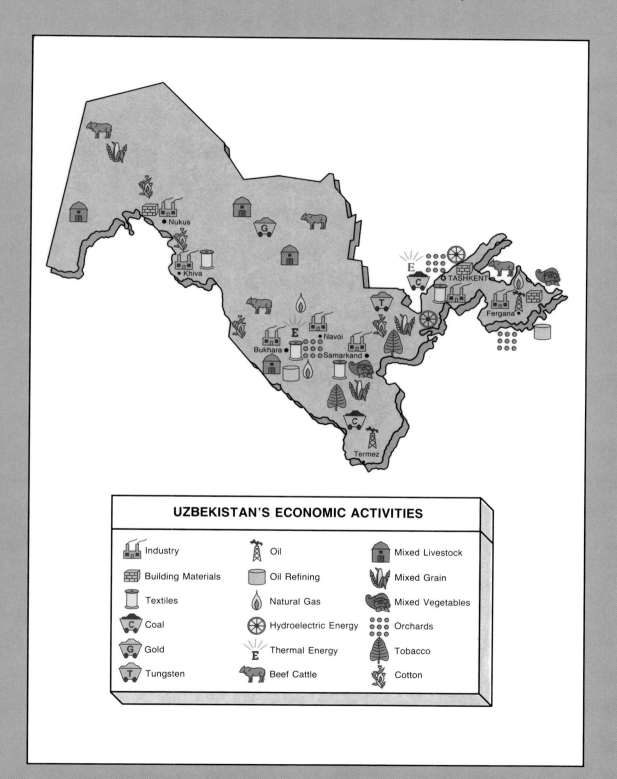

UZBEKISTAN'S ECONOMIC ACTIVITIES

Industry

Building Materials

Textiles

Coal

Gold

Tungsten

Oil

Oil Refining

Natural Gas

Hydroelectric Energy

Thermal Energy

Beef Cattle

Mixed Livestock

Mixed Grain

Mixed Vegetables

Orchards

Tobacco

Cotton

CHAPTER FOUR

What's Next for Uzbekistan?

N ow that Uzbekistan has achieved independence, it must address the issues of economic reform and environmental decline. The nation's leaders also need to establish international markets for Uzbek goods. In addition, the Uzbeks must decide what role Islam will play in the country's future. Although Uzbeks consider themselves part of the Muslim world, most citizens do not want to live in a strictly Islamic state.

Islamic countries, including Pakistan and Saudi Arabia, are keenly interested in developing cultural ties with Uzbekistan. Pakistan, for example, is helping to found mosques and madrasas, and Saudi Arabia has sent Korans and Islamic teachers to the region. Turkey, Iran, and Pakistan have also established economic agreements with Uzbekistan and with the other central Asian republics. These newly independent states now belong to regional economic zones that hope to create a common market of Islamic states. Many leaders in the area feel that modern airlines, highways, and railroads are also necessary for central Asia to prosper.

In Bukhara, boys take a break from their Islamic studies to play in the courtyard of a madrasa.

To fuel its plans for economic growth, Uzbekistan is actively seeking investment from other countries and from international banks. **Joint ventures** have been arranged with companies in Turkey, the United States, Malaysia, Indonesia, and South Korea. Other social, educational, and financial support may come from membership in world organizations, such as the **United Nations**, which Uzbekistan joined in 1992.

Another challenge to the Uzbek leadership is the continuing emigration of Russians, who make up an important class of skilled laborers and managers. Without these Russian experts, industry, health care, and education could decline. In Tashkent alone, for example, the number of Russian inhabitants has dropped by 20 percent. Although Uzbek-

INTERNATIONAL WORD GUIDE
ver. 2.1

ENGLISH	UZBEK	PRONUNCIATION
Uzbekistan	Узбекистон	uhz-bek-ihs-TAWN
Hello	Ассалому алайкум	AHS-sa-lahm-oo ah-LAY-koom
Goodbye	Хайр	KHY-ir
Please	Мархамат	mar-hah-MAT
Thank you	Рахмат	rah-MAT
Yes	Ха	HAH
No	Йук	YOK
Good	Яхши	yakh-SHEE
Bad	Ёмон	yah-MAWN

At a butcher shop in Andijan, meat — although in plentiful supply — is very expensive.

FAST FACTS ABOUT UZBEKISTAN

Total Population	21.3 million
Ethnic Mixture	71 percent Uzbek 8 percent Russian 5 percent Kazakh, Turkmen, Kyrgyz 4 percent Tajik 2 percent Karakalpak
CAPITAL and Major Cities	TASHKENT, Samarkand, Bukhara, Nukus, Khiva
Major Languages	Uzbek, Tajik
Major Religion	Islam (Sunni branch)
Year of Inclusion in USSR	1925
Status	Independent state; member of Commonwealth of Independent States since 1991 and of United Nations since 1992

istan has its own willing labor force, Uzbek workers need time to learn new job skills.

In the meantime, Uzbek scientists and journalists are urging the Russian-speaking residents in Uzbekistan to remain in the country. The Uzbeks have called for the creation of an Uzbek-Russian Friendship Society to ease ethnic tensions and to reduce the number of emigrants. In any case, joint efforts — within and outside Uzbekistan — will be necessary to ensure the country's self-sufficiency and growth.

afghanets: a dry wind that blows in southern Uzbekistan.

annex: to add a country or territory to the domain of another by force.

collective farm: a large agricultural estate worked by a group. The workers usually received a portion of the farm's harvest as wages. On a Soviet collective farm, the central government owned the land, buildings, and machinery.

Commonwealth of Independent States: a union of former Soviet republics that was created by the leaders of Russia, Belarus, and Ukraine in December 1991. The commonwealth has no formal constitution and functions as a loose economic and military association.

Communist: a person who supports Communism—an economic system in which the government owns all farmland and the means of producing goods in factories.

In Samarkand, a sculpture shows Nasredin Hodja—a legendary figure from Uzbek folklore—teaching a donkey to read the Koran (Islamic holy book).

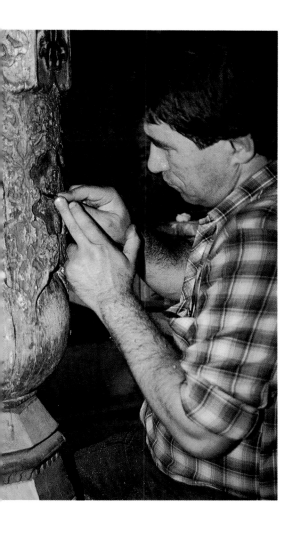

As Islam regains its importance in Uzbek life, artisans repair mosques and other buildings that were neglected or destroyed during decades of Soviet rule.

coup d'état: French words meaning "blow to the state" that refer to a swift, sudden overthrow of a government.

delimitation: the process of defining the borders of a territory.

ethnic Russian: a person whose ethnic heritage is Slavic and who speaks Russian.

ethnic Uzbek: a person whose ethnic heritage is Turkic and who speaks Uzbek.

glasnost: the Russian word for openness that refers to a Soviet policy of easing restrictions on writing and speech.

industrialize: to build and modernize factories for the purpose of manufacturing a wide variety of consumer goods and machinery.

joint venture: an economic partnership between a locally owned business and a foreign-owned company.

Karakalpak Autonomous Republic: a region that the Soviets created in 1932 and that was added to Uzbekistan in 1936.

khan: the leader of a central Asian domain, called a **khanate**, who ruled Turkic, Mongol, or Tatar peoples.

The doorway of the Tilla-Kari Madrasa in Registan Square is decorated with gold-colored tiles set in geometric designs.

protectorate: a self-governing territory under the protection and influence of a foreign power.

Russian Empire: a large kingdom ruled by czars that covered present-day Russia as well as areas to the west and south. It existed from roughly the mid-1500s to 1917.

Russian Turkestan: the western part of central Asia that the Russian Empire took over in the 19th century.

Russify: to make Russian by imposing the Russian language and culture on non-Russian peoples.

Sharia: a collection of Islamic laws based on rules of conduct in the Koran.

Turkestan Autonomous Soviet Socialist Republic: an early member of the Soviet Union that was eventually divided into five separate republics, one of which was the Uzbek Soviet Socialist Republic.

Union of Soviet Socialist Republics (USSR): a large nation in eastern Europe and northern Asia that consisted of 15 member-republics. It existed from 1922 to 1991.

United Nations: an international organization formed after World War II whose primary purpose is to promote world peace through discussion and cooperation.

An elderly vendor sells white candies at a market in Samarkand.

• *Photo Acknowledgments* •

Photographs used courtesy of: pp. 1, 38 (bottom), 46 (top), © Brynn Bruijn / *Aramco World*; pp. 5, 9 (left), 17 (left), 20 (bottom), 22 (top), 23 (top), 24 (bottom), 35, 45 (left and right), 50, © Brynn Bruijn; pp. 6, 31, © Mary Ann Brockman; pp. 2, 8 (left), 13 (bottom), 19 (right), 23 (bottom), 32 (left), 33 (left), 34 (top), 43 (right), 48, 52, 55, Ron Wixman; pp. 8 (right), 9 (right), 12 (top and bottom), 16, 17 (right), 21 (right), 22 (bottom), 25 (bottom), 26, 34 (bottom), 39, 40, 43 (left), © Yury Tatarinov; pp. 10, 13 (top), 42 (left), 44, 46 (bottom), TASS / SOVFOTO; p. 18, M. Eugene Gilliom; pp. 19 (left), 54, Marilyn Sanchez; p. 20 (top), © Tim Riley; pp. 21 (left), 36 (right), © Betty Groskin; pp. 24 (top), 53, Brian Ney; p. 25 (top), © Dennis Noonan; p. 28, The Mansell Collection; p. 30, *Chircurgie* / Guy de Chauliac; p. 32 (right), James Ford Bell Library, University of Minnesota; p. 33 (right), Metropolitan Museum of Art, Cora Timken Burnett Collection of Persian Miniatures and Other Persian Art Objects, Bequest of Cora Timken Burnett, 1956; p. 36 (left), Independent Picture Service; p. 38 (top), NOVOSTI / SOVFOTO; p. 42 (right), RIA-NOVOSTI / SOVFOTO. Maps and Charts: pp. 14-15, 47, J. Michael Roy; pp. 28-29, 50, 51, Laura Westlund, p. 37, Bryan Liedahl.

Covers: (Front) © Brynn Bruijn; (Back) Ron Wixman